WARNING TO THE NATIONS:

Throwing Out the Life Line

Mother Rose Fayton-Robinson

Warning to the Nations: 'Throwing Out the Life Line'

Scripture quotations are from The Holy Bible, English Standard Version (ESV), King James Version (KJV), New King James Version (NKJV) and New International Version (NIV)

Publisher: Inspired 4 U Publications
www.inspired4upublications.com

ISBN-13: 978-0692604632
ISBN-10: 0692604634

CONTENTS

DEDICATION

My Parents: Annie Mae and Moses Pearson

I dedicate this book to my father and mother, Moses Pearson and Annie Mae Pearson who were an inspiration in my life from day one. My mother and father were always there for me. My father was the backbone of my family who kept us in check and we were well disciplined. My mother was an anointed evangelist who held God to every promise and every Word. When the Lord told her that she was going to die, she asked Him to please allow one of her children to continue the evangelist work that He commissioned her to do. The Lord told her that it would be me and that's when Satan thought he had taken me out. I was shot in the throat and pronounced dead as a child, but God raised me from the dead and filled me with His precious Holy Ghost, Hallelujah! My mother asked me to please God and I told her that I will please God well!

I loved my parents dearly. The Bible says, *"Children, obey your parents in the Lord: for this is right. Honour thy father and mother; which is the first commandment with promise; That it may be well with thee, and thou mayest live long on the earth."* Ephesians 6:1-3 (KJV)

Mother Marjorie and Apostle John H. Boyd, Sr.

To the beloved late Founder of the New Greater Bethel Ministries in Jamaica, Queens, New York - Apostle and Pastor, Dr. John H. Boyd, Sr. – An anointed and godly man, that taught the Word of God, lived the Word of God, and who inspired me to do exactly what God has called me to do.

And to his lovely wife Mother Marjorie Boyd, thank you for praying for me daily. Your teachings and your prayers have inspired me to fulfill my assignment that God has called me to and placed on my life.

It is a joy and an honor to have served you both.

ACKNOWLEDGMENTS

I wish to express my deepest appreciation to my husband George and daughters Meltonia, Princess, Deborah, Tialia and grandchildren Toran, Trinity, Keith, II and great-grand Keith, III, my sister Mozell and brother Nathaniel. Pastor John and First Lady Valarie, Dr. Williams, Evangelist Clay, Adalia, Betty and Prophet DeCuir, and all of my sisters and brothers in Christ, my partners and friends for all of their support and prayers.

.

PREFACE

This book came directly from the Throne Room of God. It is about the second coming of Jesus Christ. He woke me up 3:00 a.m. one morning and said, "Put it in writing and make it plain. Rose, they are prostituting my pulpit. Let them know that I'm on My way back."

The word I'm giving to you today is not a word from a man, but it is a word coming directly from God's mouth to me, from my mouth to you. Take it!

I'm Throwing Out the Life Line!

"The harvest is plentiful but the workers are few."
(Matthew 9:37, NIV)

INTRODUCTION OF MOTHER ROSE
FAYTON-ROBINSON

The Mantle and the Prayer

Many years ago, my mother, Evangelist Annie Mae Pearson prayed that the work in missions and ministry our Lord and Savior had called her to would not end with her. She was a mighty woman of God and was dedicated to a life of prayer and to serving people. She traveled some, visiting the sick and praying for people who were bedridden or simply confined to their homes, but she always knew that she could have done more.

My mother loved people and was dedicated to serving in any way she could. To her, ministry was as much helping someone clean and tidy their home if they couldn't, as it was ministering to their physical ailments. Earlier in my life, she petitioned the Lord about her ministry. My mother believed that she did not do all she could for hurting people around her.

1

She had to care for her husband and small children and understood that there was so much work to be done. In Matthew 9:37-38 (NIV) the Bible says: *"The harvest is plentiful but the workers are few. Ask the Lord of the harvest, therefore, to send out workers into his harvest field."* She did just that by asking the Lord for someone to continue where she left off. He gave her the answer she desired, that it would be me, Rose. She asked God to show me in His time.

The Challenge

One day, her faith would be tested in a manner that no parent should ever experience. When I was seventeen years old, there was a knock on our front door. In an instant, my life was about to take a fatal turn, and I was completely unaware and unprepared. I had not yet accepted the Lord Jesus Christ as my personal savior.

I opened the front door and a stray bullet struck me. The bullet entered my throat and pierced my wind pipe. My mother immediately called Emergency Medical Services. You can imagine the emotions, the fear and grief that went through her. When the ambulance arrived, I was unconscious, lying in a pool of my own blood, bleeding out on my mother's floors. The medical technicians worked on me furiously, but to no avail. They pronounced me dead on arrival at the hospital. At that moment, I became a statistic, just another black teen who was shot and killed in the streets– But God!

Three doctors pronounced me dead at the hospital. My mother would not accept their report. She stood on the word of God and His promise to her that I would continue her work. She had unshakeable, complete trust in God. They tagged my toe and put a sheet over my head. These highly educated men had reached the end of their capabilities, and to them, death had won. There was nothing else they could do. Their training was no match for death.

However, when man exhausts his knowledge, and comes to the end of his own strength, it becomes an opportunity for God. Because I was dead, I do not recall any of this. I learned later that my mother refused to give up. Her faith was being tested, but she stood firm. She had a word from the Lord and she challenged death! She called out to God and reminded Him of the word He gave her; that her daughter Rose would finish the work she had started. 'Man's extremity is God's opportunity.' Each doctor did their best to convince her that it was over. My mother had great strength in God. She was not moved by what the doctors told her. I'm sure they thought she was in denial. Their words and actions did not discourage her. She believed God.

In that hospital, my mother refused to let them

take my body to the morgue. She declared, "SHE IS NOT DEAD!" At that moment, my left hand went up. Like a modern day Lazarus, I was resurrected. The doctors were stunned. They immediately took my pulse and announced, "We hear a heartbeat." The doctors said, "We need to be introduced to the God that you know!"

Evangelist Pearson believed that her call was to the Nations. The Mantle, the Purpose, the Love of People and Great Faith from God became my life's mission. My life's call is to love and help people wherever and whenever I can. This book is an extension of that Love. It is a 'Mother's Love.'

The Answer in His Time

My sister called my mother one morning. My mother had fallen while she was in the kitchen. When she called me and told me what happened, I said "I'm on my way." At that time I worked the night shift, and I immediately left my job.

My mother was my number one priority. When it concerned her, I dropped everything and tended to her. I immediately tried to book a flight, but there were no coach fares available. I didn't care about the cost so I booked a first class flight. My mother needed me and I needed to be there to care for her. You know how it is to receive that call in the middle of the night. A part of you feels helpless until you arrive and are able to see what has happened for yourself.

When I got home, she was sitting in her chair with her Bible on her chest. I was really tired, so after checking in on her and making sure she was doing well, I sat on the couch. As we were talking, I fell asleep. It seemed like I was only asleep for a few minutes before I started to dream.

In the dream, thousands of people surrounded me. I was waving my hands and people were falling out under the power of God. I woke up and sat up on the couch. My mother called me by her pet name for me and said, "Duke, what's wrong with you?" I said, "I had a dream. I was in a field waving my hand, and people were falling out and being touched by God."

My Call

My mother needed to hear that. It was God answering her prayer. She began to explain that her falling wasn't a big deal. She said, "I needed you to come so that I can tell you, as I told your sister already. I'm going to die. I asked the Lord to let one of my kids finish the work I have been doing for the Lord. You are the answer to my prayer. God answered my prayer."

She was the Pastor of a church and she was a

great evangelist. She would pray for people who the doctors gave up on and they would be healed. My mother said, "I knew the Lord said it would be you, but I asked the Lord to tell you and show you. Now I ask you to please the Lord, because I did the '*will*' of God, but I did not please Him." She said, "I'm ready to go home to Heaven and be with the Lord, so don't cry."

That day, I promised my mother that I wouldn't just please God, but I would 'well please' Him. At that time I was going to church, but I didn't allow Jesus Christ into my heart. He wasn't my savior. I was just a good church person. One day, I had purchased a brand new Lincoln car and was driving around. I heard a voice call my name. It was God calling my name. When He speaks to you, you know His voice. He said, "Rose, you will feed the hungry, clothe the poor and see that my word goes to the four corners of the earth."

Sending God's Word to the Four Corners of the Earth

One day I went to work. I worked in a hospital as a nurse assistant and as my day started, I noticed a lady was crying. I asked her, "What is wrong?" She said, "One mother can take care of 12 kids, but 12 kids cannot take care of one mother." Her response hurt my heart, so I took her home to my house for the weekend. This is where my ministry and work for God began. I had to sign her out of the hospital before I could take her home, and she never wanted to go back to the hospital. She wanted her roommate to come also; and eventually, I was able to bring her roommate home too. The next thing I knew, I had a house full of people staying in my home, and that is how I began taking care of the homeless.

The house became so crowded that I needed more space. I spoke to Apostle John H. Boyd, Sr. and he took me to a house that was a drug camp. We spoke to the owner, who agreed that we could have the house if we could get the persons out that were selling drugs. The cops would come to the house every night and the people would jump out the window. Pastor Boyd said, "We are going to get this house." The house was very dirty. We laid hands on each of the doors and prayed. We got the house. We gutted the house and fixed it up. One of our deacons at the church, Deacon Humphrey, did the electrical work on the house and this is how 'Ferndale House' for the homeless became what it is today.

One day, I was talking to my Pastor, Dr. John H. Boyd, Sr., and he said, "I think the Lord wants you to write a book." I listened to him attentively. Then he said, "The Lord will speak to you."

When the Lord began to speak to me about same

sex marriages, gays, and bi-sexual lifestyles, I organized buses and hosted a Rally on 42nd Street in Manhattan, New York. We marched and carried banners telling the world this lifestyle is wrong. We knew the message, 'WAR against Same Sex Marriages,' was not popular. However, we were not fighting a war against the people, we were fighting for the souls of men and women who may not know and understand that they were making a choice to separate themselves from God. We believed that it was important to take a stand.

THE WARNING: GOD'S HEART ABOUT SAME SEX MARRIAGE

A Mother's Love

Many of you can relate to this. A mother is truthful and honest with her children. She shares the heart of God with them. A mother instructs and warns when she sees the path her loved ones are traveling on will lead to destruction. No loving mother wants to see her children harmed. She warns, explains, pleads and cries out until her children are safe. This love is strong and does not get weary. The Bible states in 1 Corinthians 13:4-7 (NIV) *"Love is patient, love is kind. It does not envy, it does not boast, it is not proud. It does not dishonor others, it is not self-seeking, it is not easily angered, it keeps no record of wrongs. Love does not delight in evil but rejoices with the truth. It always protects, always trusts, always hopes, always perseveres."*

I share this love with you, as I discuss the heart of God concerning this very sensitive and intimate subject of same sex relationships. I am a servant of God, a lover of people, a missionary, and a mother.

I am Mother Rose Fayton-Robinson, and this is a 'Warning to the Nations'.

God's Great Love

In case you did not know this, let me be the first to tell you: *God Loves You!*

I'll say it again, "God Loves you as you are!" God's Love is unconditional. John 3:16-17 (NIV) says, *"For God so loved the world that He gave His one and only Son, that whoever believes in Him shall not perish but have eternal life. For God did not send His Son into the world to condemn the world, but to save the world through Him."*

God loves people. He created men and women in His image and His likeness. Genesis 1:26 (NIV) 'Then God said, *"Let us make mankind in our image, in our likeness..."* You and the answers to your identity are in God. If you were born a male, it is God's intention for you to be a man, and for you to marry a woman. If you were born a female, then God intends for you to be a woman, and should you choose to marry, it is God's will that you marry a man.

2 Peter 3:9 (NIV) states the Lord's intention: *"The Lord is not slow in keeping His promise, as some understand slowness. Instead He is patient with you, not*

wanting anyone to perish, but everyone to come to repentance." God does not send people to hell. You heard me? *He Is Love.* He wants the people He created to live for eternity with Him in Heaven.

God gives each and every one of us the gift of choice. He does not force us to obey Him. He presents to us a path of life and peace; a path of death and destruction. He does not trick or deceive us. He tells us what the right choice is. The rest is up to us.

The Offer

God's offer is found in Deuteronomy 30:11-20 (NIV) and it reads:

"Now what I am commanding you today is not too difficult for you or beyond your reach. [12]It is not up in heaven, so that you have to ask, "Who will ascend into heaven to get it and proclaim it to us so we may obey it. [13]Nor is it beyond the sea, so that you have to ask, "Who will cross the sea to get it and proclaim it to us so we may obey it?"

"[14]No, the word is very near you; it is in your mouth and in your heart so you may obey it.

"[15]See, I set before you today life and prosperity, death and destruction.[16]For I command you today to love the LORD your God, to walk in obedience to him, and to keep his commands, decrees and laws; then you will live and

increase, and the LORD your God will bless you in the land you are entering to possess.

"¹⁷ But if your heart turns away and you are not obedient, and if you are drawn away to bow down to other gods and worship them, ¹⁸ I declare to you this day that you will certainly be destroyed. You will not live long in the land you are crossing the Jordan to enter and possess.

"¹⁹ This day I call the heavens and the earth as witnesses against you that I have set before you life and death, blessings and curses. Now choose life, so that you and your children may live ²⁰ and that you may love the LORD your God, listen to his voice, and hold fast to him. For the LORD is your life, and he will give you many years in the land he swore to give to your fathers, Abraham, Isaac and Jacob."

The Bible is clear on the issue of same sex relations and relationships. It is a sin. Leviticus 18:22 (NKJV) says: *"You shall not lie with a male as with a woman; it is an abomination"* and Leviticus 20:13 (NKJV) says: *"If a man lies with a male as he lies with a woman, both of them have committed an abomination."* Romans 1:27 (ESV) says: *"and the men likewise gave up natural relations with women and were consumed with passion for one another, men committing shameless acts with men and receiving in themselves the due penalty for their error."*

This message is not to condemn anyone, but rather to share the heart of God concerning this subject. When Jesus was asked, what was the most important commandment?

He quoted, Deuteronomy 6:5-6 (KJV) *"⁵And thou shalt love the Lord thy God with all thine heart, and with all thy soul, and with all thy might. ⁶And these words, which I command thee this day, shall be in thine heart."*

This is my heart concerning the subject of same sex marriage, lesbianism, homosexuality, and bi-sexuality. Our war is not with people, but for people. We are first committed to loving people, and second to 'fighting the good fight of faith.'

The Lies

Let's address a few of the lies that we've heard so many times. Remember, no matter how many times a lie is repeated, does not make it right. The most common lies are: 'People can't help who they love, right?' No, this is wrong. What about: 'Gay people are born that way.' This is also a lie. We can't ignore it. People say, 'It's healthy to experiment with my sexuality.' The answer remains 'NO!' It continues, 'We're good people and we really love each other. We plan to get married, and that will make it alright.' Not so! Some may even say, 'I can't change.' These are all lies. God can change you. There is a strong power on this earth. It is the power of prayer. 1 John 1:9 (NIV) says: *"If we confess our sins, he is faithful and just and will forgive us our sins and purify us from all unrighteousness."* The 10ᵗʰ verse says, *"If we claim we have not sinned, we make him out to be a liar and His word is not in us."* 1 John 5:14-15 (NIV) assures us, *"This is the confidence we have in approaching God: that if we ask anything according to His will, he hears us. And if we know that He hears us, whatsoever we ask, we know that we have what we asked of Him."*

There is a Power available to set you free!

The Truth

The truth is that choosing to engage in a homosexual or a lesbian relationship is a matter of choice. Yes, ultimately, it is your choice. It is God's original design for a man and a woman to be joined together in Holy Matrimony before Him, and to seal this covenant by consummating the marriage creating a Holy union. Marriage, in the eyes of God, is between a man and a woman. Mark 10:6-9 (NIV) says, *"But at the beginning of creation God made them male and female. For this reason a man will leave his father and mother and be united to his wife, and the two will become one flesh. So they are no longer two, but one flesh. Therefore what God has joined together, let no one separate."*

RIGHTEOUSNESS EXALTS A NATION BUT SIN IS A REPROACH

We love our president and, as the Bible instructs us, we pray for him and all of our leaders. President Obama said he believes that the United States Constitution requires states to allow gay and lesbian couples to marry. He has stated that people should be allowed to 'love who they love.' He has supported same sex marriage from the beginning of his campaign and throughout his terms as President of the United States. When President Obama endorsed the legitimizing of same sex marriage, he brought a curse on the United States of America. Proverbs 14:34 (NIV) says, *"Righteousness exalts a nation, but sin condemns any people."* God does not change and He does not compromise!

In recent years, there has also been legislation changing laws to allow marriage between same sex partners. When this legislation was introduced, the people were allowed to vote for or against this legislation. They voted to protect the sanctity of marriage between one man and one woman. The people spoke, but their will was not respected. Instead, the same sex marriage agenda was pushed through the court system. In each state, the judge made individual rulings that allowed same sex marriage. A man can change a law, but he cannot change God's view, or the moral consequences of the sinful act. Man does not have a Heaven to put you in or a Hell to take you out of.

I read an article in the USA Today newspaper dated June 2015 about concerns of marriage. It was a marriage pledge, from DefendMarriage.org to the U.S. Supreme Court Justices, signed by tens of thousands of concerned Americans. The list included pastors, clergy, lay leaders and Jewish leaders, all asking not to be forced to choose between the state and the Laws of God. The collective affirmed that, "Any judicial opinion which purports to redefine marriage will constitute an unjust law." and they would not honor any decision that forced them to violate a clear biblical understanding of marriage as solely the union of one man and one woman.

Acts 5:29 (NKJV) *"But Peter and the other apostles answered and said: We ought to obey God rather than men."*

The Bible clearly addresses same sex relationships. God's word commands blessings and curses for His people. It is God's utmost desire to see His children blessed. Blessings come with conditions, they are not automatically given. You cannot reject the will of God and expect his blessings.

The 28th Chapter of Deuteronomy is the farewell words of instruction from the Lord to Moses for the Children of Israel before his transition. Throughout the prior 40 years, God had given them miracle after miracle since delivering them out of Egypt. He wanted to prove to His children that they could trust Him and that He would love, protect, care and provide for them.

God is a loving kind Father. Luke 12:32 (KJV) says, *"Fear not, little flock; for it is your Father's good pleasure to give you the kingdom."* In this scripture the Lord lovingly refers to us as "His flock". He uses this illustration to demonstrate how a shepherd cares for, nourishes and protects the sheep. A shepherd like our Heavenly Father can be trusted.

It shows us how tenderly God the Father loves us and shares His intentions and desires. It is our Heavenly Father's desire to give us good things, kingdom things.

Moses had to constantly remind the Israelites how God took care of them. Time after time, they disobeyed the commandments of God. It was as if, as soon as God brought them through or out of a hectic situation or a problem, they would forget their promise and turn their back on Him.

Even though they were not faithful to God, He was faithful to them. In describing God, Psalms 103:8 (KJV) says: *"The Lord is merciful and gracious, slow to anger, and plenteous in mercy."* Moses knew that sin had consequences. The 28th chapter of Deuteronomy outlines the blessings and its benefits, followed by the consequences of sin and its curses.

Moses knew that if the Israelites carefully obeyed the law, they would be a blessed nation; but, if not, they would live by the curse. That word from God is also true for us today. The Bible is the moral authority for humanity. It was written by men who received inspiration by God. It is not man's ideas or a book of good ideas.

My purpose for writing this book is to give the Father's warning and to throw out the life line to men and women around the world. Mother Rose Fayton-Robinson is *'Throwing Out the Life Line'*.

God, in His compassion and mercy, lets us know His master plan in John 3:16-17 (KJV). *"For God so loved the world that He gave His only begotten Son, that whosoever believeth in him should not perish, but have everlasting life"* [or eternal life because there is life after death]. *"For God sent not His Son into the world to condemn the world; but that the world through Him might be saved."*

In 2 Peter 3:9, the Bible also tells us that when men and women fall into sin or moral error, it is God's will that they repent, turn from their error and seek Him. God does not want anyone to perish (fall into eternal damnation). However, the Bible is absolutely clear in Roman 6:23 (NIV) *"For the wages of sin is death, but the gift of God is eternal life in Christ Jesus our Lord."*

Sodom and Gomorrah were two cities in the Bible. The sexual perversion of these two cities grieved God. You can read the account of their wickedness in Genesis the 19th chapter. God sent two angels to the city on an assignment, and the men of Sodom and Gomorrah had become so engrossed in their lust that they began to 'want and crave' after Angels. Can you imagine? The men were so carried away with lust and desire, that they formed a mob and demanded that the Angels be given to them so that they could have sex with them.

They became so aggressive that the Angels had to strike them with blindness so that they could leave the city. The wrath of God rained down fire onto the city and burned it to the ground. Everyone who live in this World will have to give an account for disobeying the laws of God.

"Start children off on the way they should go, and even when they are old they will not turn from it."

(Proverbs 22:6, NIV)

MOTHERS AND FATHERS TRAIN UP A CHILD IN THE WAY THEY SHOULD GO

Children are bombarded with sensual information, images in books and magazines, music and videos, social media and larger than life personalities that constantly engage and stimulate their natural desires and appetites. Advertisements have become seductive. These images seduce their young minds and suggest success means dressing provocatively and sexy; driving an expensive car, living an extravagant life enjoying and exploring the excess of everything to the point of ruin. For them, it is like drinking water from a gushing fire hydrant.

Parents, we are instructed to train up our children in the ways of righteousness (Proverbs 22:6). Children have a natural curiosity. We have to have straight, strong talks with them. Mothers and fathers, you have to teach your children godly principles so that they can recognize evil and ungodliness.

While in prayer, the Holy Spirit told me, "This generation needs you." He instructed me to show them love, be there for them, listen to them, hug and talk to them.

Parents, I offer you these guidelines:

1. Raise your child on biblical principles, which are unchanging and eternal, and which are not based on man-made laws that change to accommodate a generation seeking pleasure.

2. Don't allow the homosexual, lesbian, gay, or bi-sexual agenda to be pushed on your children. Legislature is refusing to allow prayer in school, but is fighting for sexually confusing information to be taught to young children.

3. Protect and guard them. Monitor what they watch on television, listen to on the radio, and are exposed to on the computer by way of social media, advertising and unsolicited emails. Watch your children, monitor and protect them while they are young and very impressionable. When they are older, guide them with the word of God and keep it before them.

4. Teach your children what the Bible says about marriage between one man and one woman. The government and society hold parents accountable for the welfare of their children. There are penalties for contributing to the delinquency of a minor. However, in contradiction, the same government endorses the teaching of a 'mixed and alternate sexual agenda'. It is wrong to teach a child that a same sex relationship is acceptable and natural when the Bible clearly teaches that it is an abomination.

5. Pray for your children and teach them to pray.

6. Love your children, and show them love and affection.

7. Take your children to church. Encourage them to develop godly friendships. Support the Youth Leaders in your community and churches.

Moms and dads, your children need you to be godly parents. The best support you can give your children is to be active in their lives. Don't be afraid of talking and addressing complex issues. Give honest answers based on biblical principles. Do not waiver. Most of all let your light shine before them.

I was on a plane and when I sat down, I opened a Bible. When I opened my Bible, the young girl sitting next to me got up and left. She never returned. There were a few vacant seats so she moved herself. I thought she had went to the restroom until I noticed she never returned to her seat.

The plane began to experience air pockets and turbulence. I sat there calmly reading my Bible. The young lady came back to her seat and asked, "What is wrong with you? Why are you so calm?" Everyone on the plane was clearly upset and full of fear. I said to her, "There is nothing wrong with me." She asked, "Why aren't you scared?" I said, "The plane is not going down." She could not understand how I could know that. I told her, "Because I'm on this plane." She said, "What does that mean?" I said, "It means I am a child of King Jesus and this plane is not going down!" She wanted to know how I got that kind of faith and belief in God. I asked her if she went to church. She said, "No, but I want that kind of belief. I want strong faith in God." I asked her, "Would you like to be saved?" She said, "If I can have that kind of faith, I want it." She accepted Christ in her heart.

We are commanded to let our light shine before men, so that they can see our good works and glorify our Father in Heaven (Matthew 5:16). The final instructions I gave her were: "Pray. Ask God to direct you to a church and join a good church that teaches God's word."

WARNING TO PREACHERS

My mother dreamt that the Lord took her to hell. While she was there, she saw so many preachers in hell, screaming and crying. As she looked around, she realized she knew many of them. She never told me who she saw; the Lord would not allow her to speak on it.

My mother told me to never go to church without a Bible. She said to be sure that the messages preached are from the Bible. Many preachers are preaching from history books, the newspaper, and the nightly news. They are preaching what's popular and labeling themselves as life coaches. Preachers, "Preach the word of God! Do not compromise God's word."

Pastors and ministers are compromising and teaching false doctrine. A Bishop who once taught God's word is now teaching that it is alright to be homosexual or a lesbian and go to Heaven. He said he had a revelation about inclusion. This is false doctrine. God's word is not complicated. Obey what the Bible says.

Another female Bishop married her lesbian lover in another state, returned and continued to preach every Sunday. She said she talked it over with her lover who is also in ministry and they could not find in the Holy Bible where lesbianism is wrong.

A gospel recording artist announced that he was gay. He was married to a woman, the marriage ended, and now he is with a man. He said he is the same person he has always been when he was singing popular gospel songs. He said God wants him in a committed relationship, and it does not matter if it's with a man.

There is a gay couple that pastors a church. They are referred to as Bishop and First Man. I ask you, "What Bible are they teaching from?" The gospel of Jesus did not permit relationships between two men. They are in error. Do not follow these people and do not allow them to convince you that something is right when the Bible clearly tells you it is wrong.

Churches are changing and are allowing homosexual bishops, priests, pastors and teachers. They are giving in to the pressure from the world to be politically correct. These people will be held accountable for their actions and for leading people to error. The Bible is clear that homosexuality and lesbianism are against the will of God. Preachers stand up and preach the Gospel.

The Lord woke me up at 3:00 in the morning. He said, "Rose, they are prostituting my pulpit." Preachers, you need to get your soul and spirit in order. He said, "Ministers need to sell out. They need to completely surrender all of their heart, soul, mind, and body. They need to stop playing church. They can't tell the congregation one thing and live another." God is not dead. He is alive and well. He sees everything. Nothing gets by God's eyes unnoticed.

When the Lord saved me, I surrendered my all to Him. I remembered my first husband, who is deceased now. He used to host the men from the local church in our basement. Deacons used to come over, sit around and drink liquor. My husband bought the good stuff and he stocked enough of it for all the men to drink as much as they like. That bothered me. I took a hatchet, went down to the basement and "hatchered" the bar and all the liquor. I know that's not a word, but it fits. After I tore out the bar, I poured the entire stock of that top shelf liquor down the drain. I got rid of it! My husband knew change had taken place in me. I could not allow our home to be used to support drinking and whatever else goes along with it.

Pastors, prophets, evangelists, apostles, and

teachers repent and come back to God. Hell is a wide road. You cannot get into the pulpit and preach well by allowing people to do what they want to do. You are doing wrong and you allow them to do wrong because they are bringing in plenty of money to the church. Their blood will be on your hands. Wrong is wrong and right is right! We have reached the point where we don't know wrong from right.

Now I know why my mother said to me, "Don't ever go to church without a Bible. You must read the truth for yourself." When the Lord allowed my mother to go down into hell in a vision, she saw all of these preachers in those little dim churches, trying to pray themselves out of hell. While they were alive, their light in ministry had almost completely gone out. In hell, they were trying to make things right to try to get out or get a second chance. But only what you do here on earth will count. There is no work beyond the grave. And hell has no exit. If you go to hell, you are there to stay for all eternity.

My mother walked all over hell. The preachers in hell were trying to keep her down there. They could not escape. This is not God's will. 2 Peter 3:9 shows us God's will towards mankind. He does not want anyone to perish. His desire is that everyone should repent. Today, listen to the warning. The time to choose is now. Choose life and peace!

Ministers read your Bible and cover yourself with

the blood of Jesus. The blood of Jesus is your safety zone. Take His Holy Communion, and preach the gospel!

"This day I call the heavens and the earth as witnesses against you that I have set before you life and death, blessings and curses. Now choose life, so that you and your children may live…"

(Deuteronomy 30:19, NIV)

THROWING OUT THE LIFE LINE

My mother always told me whatever you sow, you will reap. Galatians 6:7-8 (NIV) says it also: *"Do not be deceived: God cannot be mocked. A man reaps what he sows. Whoever sows to please their flesh, from the flesh will reap destruction; whoever sows to please the Spirit, from the Spirit will reap eternal life."*

Do you know that for every decision you make, there is a consequence? You can't do things just because you are able to do it. It will come back to you. Pray before you make your decisions and use the Bible to guide you, it is your road map. We are in a dangerous stage. This world needs to turn back to God. We have withdrawn ourselves from the protection of the Most High God.

Can you stop yourself from dying? No. That should let you know there is a Higher Power. His name is Jesus. Listen men and women, "I'm throwing out the life line." A day will come, if you

31

live long enough, when you will get old. Your health, vitality and appearance may fail, and your money may even fail. Is that the way you want to face Jesus, without hope and without the assurance of eternal life? Ask for forgiveness for all of your wrong doings. The greatest discovery is the Love of Jesus which was demonstrated by his act on the cross. This is the only power that transforms man.

I'm not writing this book to make you feel ashamed or bad. I am writing this book to give you a chance to repent. It is not if you die, but 'when you die'. There is nothing that you can do about it. The Bible lets us know that people are destined to die once and after that, to face judgment (Hebrews 9:27). You can be sure that the Bible is true about these two things: First, you will die; and second, you will stand before God to be judged.

If you welcome the Lord Jesus into your heart, you will spend your eternity with Jesus Christ. Romans 10:9–10 (NIV): *"If you declare with your mouth, "Jesus is Lord," and believe in your heart that God raised Him from the dead, you will be saved. For it is with your heart that you believe and are justified, and it is with your mouth that you profess your faith and are saved."*

If you reject this message and Christ, you will spend eternity in Hell. There will be no parties. Hell is a place of eternal damnation and torment. Choose Life and Peace. Choose Christ.

A TESTIMONY OF DELIVERANCE

"I was born November 15, 1960. When I was a child as young as 3 until the age of 17, I was molested by my father. I always felt something had happened to me because I began liking girls at 5 years old and had fantasies about touching and kissing them. The first woman I had a crush on was my own mother. To me, she was the most beautiful woman in the world. She was like Halle Berry- just FINE! Anyway, when I was 25, I got into my first gay relationship with a 15 year old. Her parents approved of the relationship.

When I turned 35, God called my name and said, "It's time." I stopped smoking. One Sunday, God said, "Ethel, I will change you this Friday." Well, He did it! I made it through those days and God changed me. He told me I had to give away all my men's clothing and he would give me new clothes. I saved one outfit and wore those clothes for 2 weeks. Then, I was taken to a church by Sister

Pearl and led into a room full of clothes, shoes, and coats. "Take what you want," she told me. LOOK AT GOD! He provided a room that supplied all I had given away.

I asked God, "Why can't I stay gay and go to Heaven?" The Holy Spirit led me to Romans 1:18-32 (NIV), *"¹⁸The wrath of God is being revealed from heaven against all the godlessness and wickedness of people, who suppress the truth by their wickedness, ¹⁹ since what may be known about God is plain to them, because God has made it plain to them. ²⁰ For since the creation of the world God's invisible qualities—his eternal power and divine nature— have been clearly seen, being understood from what has been made, so that people are without excuse.*

²¹ For although they knew God, they neither glorified him as God nor gave thanks to him, but their thinking became futile and their foolish hearts were darkened. ²² Although they claimed to be wise, they became fools ²³ and exchanged the glory of the immortal God for images made to look like a mortal human being and birds and animals and reptiles.

²⁴ Therefore God gave them over in the sinful desires of their hearts to sexual impurity for the degrading of their bodies with one another. ²⁵ They exchanged the truth about God for a lie, and worshiped and served created things rather than the Creator—who is forever praised. Amen.

²⁶ Because of this, God gave them over to shameful lusts. Even their women exchanged natural sexual relations for unnatural ones. ²⁷ In the same way the men also abandoned natural relations with women and were inflamed with lust for one another. Men committed shameful acts with other men, and received in themselves the due penalty for their error.

"[28] Furthermore, just as they did not think it worthwhile to retain the knowledge of God, so God gave them over to a depraved mind, so that they do what ought not to be done. [29] They have become filled with every kind of wickedness, evil, greed and depravity. They are full of envy, murder, strife, deceit and malice. They are gossips, [30] slanderers, God-haters, insolent, arrogant and boastful; they invent ways of doing evil; they disobey their parents; [31] they have no understanding, no fidelity, no love, no mercy. [32] Although they know God's righteous decree that those who do such things deserve death, they not only continue to do these very things but also approve of those who practice them."

In His word, I found truth that spoke to my heart and soul. God delivered me from being a Dyke or an *AG, as they say, to being a virtuous woman of God and a witness of His truth to others. But then, I was drawn back into that lifestyle again and lived with another partner. The enemy tried to destroy me when I almost took my life because of that relationship ... But God delivered me once again!

Yes, God loves us. But, He is not pleased with that lifestyle. God's word remains the same in the New and Old Testament. If God was alright with this homosexual lifestyle, then He would have left me the way I was. But, to God be the Glory! I was made whole again, a virtuous woman of God! Hallelujah!" – Ethel T.

*AG – The Urban Dictionary describes the term as follows: (ag-dyke) an aggressive dyke who shows too much cleavage for guys to gawk at but only girls can look at them.

THE BIBLICAL BLESSING OF OBEDIENCE AND THE CURSE OF DISOBEDIENCE

Deuteronomy 28:1-68 (KJV)

"And it shall come to pass, if thou shalt hearken diligently unto the voice of the LORD thy God, to observe and to do all his commandments which I command thee this day, that the LORD thy God will set thee on high above all nations of the earth: ²And all these blessings shall come on thee, and overtake thee, if thou shalt hearken unto the voice of the LORD thy God. ³Blessed shalt thou be in the city, and blessed shalt thou be in the field. ⁴Blessed shall be the fruit of thy body, and the fruit of thy ground, and the fruit of thy cattle, the increase of thy kine, and the flocks of thy sheep. ⁵Blessed shall be thy basket and thy store. ⁶Blessed shalt thou be when thou comest in, and blessed shalt thou be when thou goest out.

"[7] The LORD shall cause thine enemies that rise up against thee to be smitten before thy face: they shall come out against thee one way, and flee before thee seven ways. [8] The LORD shall command the blessing upon thee in thy storehouses, and in all that thou settest thine hand unto; and he shall bless thee in the land which the LORD thy God giveth thee. [9] The LORD shall establish thee an holy people unto himself, as he hath sworn unto thee, if thou shalt keep the commandments of the LORD thy God, and walk in his ways. [10] And all people of the earth shall see that thou art called by the name of the LORD; and they shall be afraid of thee.

"[11] And the LORD shall make thee plenteous in goods, in the fruit of thy body, and in the fruit of thy cattle, and in the fruit of thy ground, in the land which the LORD sware unto thy fathers to give thee. [12] The LORD shall open unto thee his good treasure, the heaven to give the rain unto thy land in his season, and to bless all the work of thine hand: and thou shalt lend unto many nations, and thou shalt not borrow. [13] And the LORD shall make thee the head, and not the tail; and thou shalt be above only, and thou shalt not be beneath; if that thou hearken unto the commandments of the LORD thy God, which I command thee this day, to observe and to do them: [14] And thou shalt not go aside from any of the words which I command thee this day, to the right hand, or to the left, to go after other gods to serve them.

"¹⁵ But it shall come to pass, if thou wilt not hearken unto the voice of the LORD thy God, to observe to do all his commandments and his statutes which I command thee this day; that all these curses shall come upon thee, and overtake thee: ¹⁶ Cursed shalt thou be in the city, and cursed shalt thou be in the field. ¹⁷ Cursed shall be thy basket and thy store. ¹⁸ Cursed shall be the fruit of thy body, and the fruit of thy land, the increase of thy kine, and the flocks of thy sheep. ¹⁹ Cursed shalt thou be when thou comest in, and cursed shalt thou be when thou goest out. ²⁰ The LORD shall send upon thee cursing, vexation, and rebuke, in all that thou settest thine hand unto for to do, until thou be destroyed, and until thou perish quickly; because of the wickedness of thy doings, whereby thou hast forsaken me.

"²¹ The LORD shall make the pestilence cleave unto thee, until he have consumed thee from off the land, whither thou goest to possess it. ²² The LORD shall smite thee with a consumption, and with a fever, and with an inflammation, and with an extreme burning, and with the sword, and with blasting, and with mildew; and they shall pursue thee until thou perish. ²³ And thy heaven that is over thy head shall be brass, and the earth that is under thee shall be iron. ²⁴ The LORD shall make the rain of thy land powder and dust: from heaven shall it come down upon thee, until thou be destroyed. ²⁵ The LORD shall cause thee to be smitten before thine enemies: thou shalt go out one way against them, and flee seven ways before them: and shalt be removed into all the kingdoms of the earth. [26] And thy carcase shall be meat unto all fowls of the air, and unto the beasts of the earth, and no man shall fray them away.

"[27] The LORD will smite thee with the botch of Egypt, and with the emerods, and with the scab, and with the itch, whereof thou canst not be healed. [28] The LORD shall smite thee with madness, and blindness, and astonishment of heart: [29] And thou shalt grope at noonday, as the blind gropeth in darkness, and thou shalt not prosper in thy ways: and thou shalt be only oppressed and spoiled evermore, and no man shall save thee. [30] Thou shalt betroth a wife, and another man shall lie with her: thou shalt build an house, and thou shalt not dwell therein: thou shalt plant a vineyard, and shalt not gather the grapes thereof.

"[31] Thine ox shall be slain before thine eyes, and thou shalt not eat thereof: thine ass shall be violently taken away from before thy face, and shall not be restored to thee: thy sheep shall be given unto thine enemies, and thou shalt have none to rescue them. [32] Thy sons and thy daughters shall be given unto another people, and thine eyes shall look, and fail with longing for them all the day long; and there shall be no might in thine hand. [33] The fruit of thy land, and all thy labours, shall a nation which thou knowest not eat up; and thou shalt be only oppressed and crushed alway: [34] So that thou shalt be mad for the sight of thine eyes which thou shalt see.

"³⁵ The LORD shall smite thee in the knees, and in the legs, with a sore botch that cannot be healed, from the sole of thy foot unto the top of thy head. ³⁶ The LORD shall bring thee, and thy king which thou shalt set over thee, unto a nation which neither thou nor thy fathers have known; and there shalt thou serve other gods, wood and stone. ³⁷ And thou shalt become an astonishment, a proverb, and a byword, among all nations whither the LORD shall lead thee. ³⁸ Thou shalt carry much seed out into the field, and shalt gather but little in; for the locust shall consume it. ³⁹ Thou shalt plant vineyards, and dress them, but shalt neither drink of the wine, nor gather the grapes; for the worms shall eat them.

"⁴⁰ Thou shalt have olive trees throughout all thy coasts, but thou shalt not anoint thyself with the oil; for thine olive shall cast his fruit. ⁴¹ Thou shalt beget sons and daughters, but thou shalt not enjoy them; for they shall go into captivity. ⁴² All thy trees and fruit of thy land shall the locust consume. ⁴³ The stranger that is within thee shall get up above thee very high; and thou shalt come down very low. ⁴⁴ He shall lend to thee, and thou shalt not lend to him: he shall be the head, and thou shalt be the tail.

"⁴⁵ Moreover all these curses shall come upon thee, and shall pursue thee, and overtake thee, till thou be destroyed; because thou hearkenedst not unto the voice of the LORD thy God, to keep his commandments and his statutes which he commanded thee: ⁴⁶ And they shall be upon thee for

a sign and for a wonder, and upon thy seed for ever.
[47] Because thou servedst not the LORD thy God with
joyfulness, and with gladness of heart, for the
abundance of all things; [48] Therefore shalt thou serve
thine enemies which the LORD shall send against
thee, in hunger, and in thirst, and in nakedness, and
in want of all things: and he shall put a yoke of iron
upon thy neck, until he have destroyed thee.

"[49] The LORD shall bring a nation against thee from
far, from the end of the earth, as swift as the eagle
flieth; a nation whose tongue thou shalt not
understand; [50] A nation of fierce countenance, which
shall not regard the person of the old, nor shew
favour to the young: [51] And he shall eat the fruit of
thy cattle, and the fruit of thy land, until thou be
destroyed: which also shall not leave thee either
corn, wine, or oil, or the increase of thy kine, or
flocks of thy sheep, until he have destroyed thee.
[52] And he shall besiege thee in all thy gates, until thy
high and fenced walls come down, wherein thou
trustedst, throughout all thy land: and he shall
besiege thee in all thy gates throughout all thy land,
which the LORD thy God hath given thee.

"[53] And thou shalt eat the fruit of thine own body,
the flesh of thy sons and of thy daughters, which the
LORD thy God hath given thee, in the siege, and in
the straitness, wherewith thine enemies shall distress
thee: [54] So that the man that is tender among you,
and very delicate, his eye shall be evil toward his
brother, and toward the wife of his bosom, and

toward the remnant of his children which he shall leave: [55] So that he will not give to any of them of the flesh of his children whom he shall eat: because he hath nothing left him in the siege, and in the straitness, wherewith thine enemies shall distress thee in all thy gates. [56] The tender and delicate woman among you, which would not adventure to set the sole of her foot upon the round for delicateness and tenderness, her eye shall be evil toward the husband of her bosom, and toward her son, and toward her daughter, [57] And toward her young one that cometh out from between her feet, and toward her children which she shall bear: for she shall eat them for want of all things secretly in the siege and straitness, wherewith thine enemy shall distress thee in thy gates.

"[58] If thou wilt not observe to do all the words of this law that are written in this book, that thou mayest fear this glorious and fearful name, THE LORD THY GOD; [59] Then the LORD will make thy plagues wonderful, and the plagues of thy seed, even great plagues, and of long continuance, and sore sicknesses, and of long continuance. [60] Moreover he will bring upon thee all the diseases of Egypt, which thou wast afraid of; and they shall cleave unto thee. [61] Also every sickness, and every plague, which is not written in the book of this law, them will the LORD bring upon thee, until thou be destroyed. [62] And ye shall be left few in number, whereas ye were as the stars of heaven for multitude; because thou wouldest not obey the voice of the LORD thy God.

"⁶³ And it shall come to pass, that as the LORD rejoiced over you to do you good, and to multiply you; so the LORD will rejoice over you to destroy you, and to bring you to nought; and ye shall be plucked from off the land whither thou goest to possess it. ⁶⁴ And the LORD shall scatter thee among all people, from the one end of the earth even unto the other; and there thou shalt serve other gods, which neither thou nor thy fathers have known, even wood and stone. ⁶⁵ And among these nations shalt thou find no ease, neither shall the sole of thy foot have rest: but the LORD shall give thee there a trembling heart, and failing of eyes, and sorrow of mind:

"⁶⁶ And thy life shall hang in doubt before thee; and thou shalt fear day and night, and shalt have none assurance of thy life: ⁶⁷ In the morning thou shalt say, Would God it were even! and at even thou shalt say, Would God it were morning! for the fear of thine heart wherewith thou shalt fear, and for the sight of thine eyes which thou shalt see. ⁶⁸ And the LORD shall bring thee into Egypt again with ships, by the way whereof I spake unto thee, Thou shalt see it no more again: and there ye shall be sold unto your enemies for bondmen and bondwomen, and no man shall buy you."

CLOSING PRAYERS & INVITATION

Lord, I give you all the thanks, all the praises and honor; all of it belongs to you. Thank you for making me worthy to write this book in your honor. You told me one day that you would hand pick me. Now Lord, I pray that the meditation of your Word would sink into the heart of man and that they would live a life pleasing to you and run for the mark of the high calling, that mark is King Jesus!

Beloved, I pray that my 'Throwing Out the Life Line' has been a blessing and inspiration for you to draw closer to God. God specializes in love, grace and mercy. He specializes in listening to your cry and prayer. God specializes in deliverance, and in restoring, reviving and renewing a right spirit within our hearts that we may not sin against Him or others by word, thought or deed. He specializes in restoring us back to how He originally created us, in

His image. Be encouraged to let the purpose, plan and will of God be done in your life. Study the Word of God daily. God loves you and so do I!

The Invitation

I hope you will run to Jesus with everything you have. I tell you once and I tell you again, there is still room at the altar, and a loving Savior is waiting to wrap His arms around you.

Jesus Christ is the Only Way, as stated in John 14:6 (NIV) *Jesus answered, "I am the way and the truth and the life. No one comes to the Father except through me."*

If you have not yet accepted Jesus Christ into your precious heart and life, I invite you to open your heart and welcome Him in at this time.

Please accept Christ into your Heart.

ABOUT THE AUTHOR

Rose Fayton–Robinson, affectionately called "Mother Fayton," is founder and facilitator of the patient homecare facility 'Ferndale House' and the President and CEO of "The Mother Rose Fayton-Robinson Foundation." Her efforts, concern and love for people have grown into three (3) facilities. These facilities house males and females of various ages and spectrums of life that include teenagers to the elderly, who are physically disabled, mentally ill, and battered.

Mother Fayton started patient homecare almost

30 years ago at her home in Hollis, NY when she invited a displaced patient at the hospital where she worked to her house for the weekend. This incident paved the way for Ferndale House, which became the chief cornerstone for her foundation.

Mother Fayton's enlarged commitment is not only dedicated to the Ferndale Houses, but extends to her service as the head of the New Greater Bethel Ministries Pastoral Care Committee and overseer of Concerned Positive Women which is a ministry designed to build and encourage women. Her life experiences, leadership abilities, and excellent organizational skills make her a pillar in her niche and a "go to" person for all who have made her acquaintance.

Mother Fayton started employment at the state hospital, Creedmoor Psychiatric Center. Unbeknownst to her, this was the beginning of a lifetime commitment in the mental health and social work field. She believes that *"In this natural life, nothing will flourish without a seed being planted and nourished."* Reflecting back on her unforeseen blessing, she remembers her mother's love for people and how she herself used to take care of neighborhood people during her childhood. Among her many attributes, she is a beloved true child of God, whose selfless contributions have touched many lives.

Mother Rose Fayton-Robinson can be contacted

for speaking engagements, discount book orders, questions and comments at:
motherrosebooks@gmail.com

"For God so loved the world that he gave his one and only Son, that whoever believes in him shall not perish but have eternal life."

(John 3:16, NIV)

WORKS CITED

ESV: The Holy Bible, English Standard Version Copyright © 2001 by Crossway Bibles, a publishing ministry of Good News Publishers.

KJV: Scripture quotations from The Authorized (King James) Version. Rights in the Authorized Version in the United Kingdom are vested in the Crown. Reproduced by permission of the Crown a patentee, Cambridge University Press.

NIV: The Holy Bible, New International Version®, NIV® Copyright ©1973, 1978, 1984, 2011 by Biblica, Inc.® Used by permission. All rights reserved worldwide.

NKJV: New King James Version®. Copyright © 1982 by Thomas Nelson. Used by permission. All rights reserved.

Testimony by Ethel T.

USA Today June 2015 www.defendmarriage.org.

www.urbandictionary.com.